Straight James / Gay James

Books by James Franco

Actors Anonymous
A California Childhood
Strongest of the Litter
Rebel
Dangerous Book Four Boys
Palo Alto
Directing Herbert White
New Film Stills
Moving Pictures/Moving Sculptures
Hollywood Dreaming
Magic Mountain/Home Movies

Straight James / Gay James

James Franco

H P G

HANSEN PUBLISHING GROUP, LLC

Straight James / Gay James
Copyright © 2016 Whose Dog R U Productions, Inc.

22 21 20 19 18 17 16   1 2 3 4 5 6

ISBN: *978-1-60182-262-8 (trade paper)*
       978-1-60182-263-5 (ebook)

This book is a work of fiction. Names, character, places, and incidents either are products of the author's imagination or are used fictitiously. Any resemblance to actual events or locales or persons, living or dead, is entirely coincidental.

Every effort has been made to correctly attribute all material reproduced in this book. If any error has been made unwittingly, we will be happy to correct it in future editions.

Permission acknowledgments appear on page 57.

Book design by Jon Hansen

Cover design by Gregg Barrios

Cover art by Cheyenne Randall

Author photograph by Anna Kooris; tattoo art by Cheyenne Randall

Hansen Publishing Group, LLC
302 Ryders Lane,
East Brunswick, NJ 08816

http://hansenpublishing.com

To the music of Lana Del Rey.

I've got a war in my mind.

—Lana Del Rey

CONTENTS

Straight James / Gay James

DUMBO

Dumb is me,
As a young elephant I was shy,
From too much attention,
So, speak I didn't.

A young animal:
At age thirteen, life plunked
Me down in junior high,
Like Dumbo in the circus.

As I grew,
Isolation followed me
And the only recourse
Was to drink hard with the clowns.

Pink elephants
Paraded and sloshed
Through my youth
Until I became a sinister clown,

With a smile painted
So thick
I looked mad-happy, always.
And I never flew,

I never flew.

MASK

There is a face,
And it's mine.
It is a mask I wear,
And money comes.

White, young, lusty, Sym-
Metrical, dark browed;
This mask is the face
Of Gucci, officially.

Because this mask
Has been branded,
My face underneath,
The one they call "me,"

Can be a naughty face.
He is the face
That drips with cum,
And glistens with pussy.

A secret devil
Beneath
The slick surface
Of the Gucci smile.

All I have to do
To keep this double
Reign of outer Poster
Boy and inner Beezle

Is keep these creatures
Separate,
So they don't mix
In public,

While at night,
In sparkly light
They are but
One: me.

CUSTOM HOTEL

There is a hotel on the edge of Los Angeles
Near the airport on Lincoln, its title is high,
And red, above the traffic bound to LAX,
Slugging through the Inglewood smog:

Custom Hotel it says above, oven hot red.

Unlike the regular airport hotels
The Custom has a little bit of comfort
And style—behind the check-in desk,
Five monitors, showing in slow-mo,

Different scenes of Los Angeles:
Skateboarders gliding in the cement bowls
Under the palm trees of Venice; *Traffic,*
Seen from above, and in a trick of the edit,

Driving backwards on the hot,
Rubber scarred
Freeway—sucked back
By a force as powerful as God.

On the fourth: the spinning blue globe
Of "The Crossroads of the World;"
On the fifth, surfers surfing,
The ocean crashing.

*

I come through here *every* week,
The last stop before the airport-launch-pad,
Back to wherever the cameras need me.
I always get number 1212.

It looks to the airport and beyond to water.
Before dusk the view burns into desaturated
Fuchsia, with the grain of old eight millimeter,
—A nineteen seventies home movie sunset.

The white sun drops below
The West Side horizon
Like a baby in a chrisom,
Baptized in a sky of blood.

At night: a centipede of lights.

*

These are my Wicked, Wicked Ways,
I am the Witch King of the Hollywood Hills,
The dark star rising: Hollywood Actor.
Pretty things see me on the screen,

And then I step out of the screen
And take them in their petrified awe.
I take the wise ones too,
But they are of my coven.

I know my own Satanic strength,
And I check it with good will,
Giving back the charity of my experience,
Growing little actor gardens, here and there.

Flowers bloom, and flowers fade.

*

Blonde hair climbed
Under the shower with me,
We kissed on our knees
In the blue water,

Then out to the bed,
The red light from the Custom sign
In through the window,
Redding everything.

Beyond, the planes
Lift, as if on strings,
Above the black damped city.
And the red sign backlights

Her shoulders like devil's wings.

THE GUCCI BOOK OF THE DEAD

King Tut had his Tomb
Full of all his earthly things,
To keep him happy
In the Land of the Dead.

Servants, killed; dogs, sacrificed;
Herbs, spices, ceremonial masks;
His preserved entrails,
And mummified brain,

Transferred to the other side.

Bury me in my Gooch,
Entomb me in cooch;
Leather jacket, by damn,
Denim close on ham;

Boots of the Devil,
Hair of a widow's peak;
Young women to serve,
Cats, and kittens to pet,

This is how I'll live in Beyond.

The *Gucci Book Of The Dead*
States that Living is Style,
And therefore Dying is Style,
And the Devil is in the Details;

I would make a Heaven of Hell
With a few well chosen accessories:
Black Jacket to hold my Red Wings,
Black Boots for my Cloven Hooves,

Black Shades for Eyes that Burn.

BLACK DEATH

I put on the mask of Richard Ramirez
And drive through these poems
Like a Satanic killer cruising down
The 1980s Los Angeles freeways

At night, in a stolen car, high on speed,
Highway to Hell on the stereo.
AC/DC baseball cap: On. Avia high tops:
On. Black trench coat: On.

I once was a robber, now I'm a robber
Of souls. Think about it, and nightmare:
You wake; I'm over you, your wife:
Next to you; a gun in your face, you're dead.

I've snuck into your house,
It was so isolated, on your quiet street,
No one noticed me, stealthy
As the Angel of Death, my coattails

Spread like black wings.
There was a marking on your door,
Not lamb's blood, but an invisible
Sign, that only I could read. It said: victims.

I've killed you. I spend hours with your wife.

GOAT BOY

"Goat Boy" is the cobbled together remains of a student short film based on a poem by Frank Bidart called "Herbert White." These are the bits that were taken out because I didn't need the backstory for the title character of that film, also named "Herbert White," played by the great and strange Michael Shannon of *Boardwalk Empire.*

*

"Goat Boy" is the backstory provided by Frank to fill out Herbert. The funny thing is that Herbert is a killer and a necrophiliac, but Frank gives him some of his own life experience as backstory, meaning Herbert is a mask under which Frank has put his own beating heart, his own feeling body, his own clenched teeth, and his tears.

*

The part about the father, that's Frank's father. His father is a ghost who haunts the Bakersfield of Frank's poetry. The Goat, that's Herbert's. There was something or other about fucking goats in that book Frank used as inspiration: *21 Abnormal Sex Cases.* You see? It's in there, in the movie.

*

All those little goats, they're cute, eh? We shot them running around their pen the morning after the wrap party in Suffolk, Virginia. The focus puller, Chris, was hungover. We chased them around their little pen on a farm full of animals. Nearby, when I went to piss, I passed a kennel full of dogs, the loudest and biggest was an overgrown hound dog, as big as a horse, with red veiny eyes, and a corrupt mouth, speckled, pink and black — gouty with dropsy — barking incessantly, an evil booming echo, again and again, the hope-killing base-call of the hound of hell.

These actors are all Virginians, found locally at a casting call. Think of the hundreds that lined up to be in the film: children, teens, parents. Some shy, some drunk. These were the ones we chose. The father, played by Cody from Richmond—home of Poe—was in a band with Ginsberg, The Fugs. He also acted in *Child of God,* as one of the hunters who pulls one-armed Lester from the hospital bed, alongside an actual con man who conned one of my employees into an almost-marriage, and stole a rifle-gun from a Texan. In *Child of God,* Cody's grumbled answer to Lester's question about where they're taking him: "We're going to your funeral, motherfucker."

*

"Man's spunk is the salt of the earth."

*

Man's spunk is the salt of the earth and it makes things grow. True enough. How to make sense of it? In a poem it's one thing, in a movie it's another.

*

In the poem the boy fucks a goat, and it gets strangled on its rope, then he jerks off on it to bring it back to life. In the film, because it's time based, and because climaxes in film—both dramatic and sexual—work differently than in a poem, we didn't have him fuck the goat, because it would then be anti-climactic to have him jerk off on the goat. We had him kill the goat out of anger, and then jerk off on it. Because, *man's spunk is the salt of the earth and it makes things grow.*

21

*

We didn't really kill the goat, we had a vet on hand who put it under for ten minutes so it would look dead.

*

Movie magic.

*

Near where we shot the goat was a turkey that was so fat it couldn't stand; its disgusting red, and blue head, dripping with excess skin, like an old man's monstrous phallus, sprouting from a blob of molten feathers. It made me swear off turkey sandwiches for half a year.

*

I took the clips that were left over from "Herbert White," put them together, and then zoomed in on everything. Everything is super close and fucked up. Weird frames.

I WAS BORN INTO A WORLD

I was born into a world
Before recycling was a thing,

Before oil wars,
When the biggest world

Threat was nuclear.
The only extinct thing

Was the Dodo,
We consumed and junked.

Then we were told about
Droughts, and disappearing

Rainforests.
About melting ice caps,

And we fought Iraq
For a second time,

Like father like son,
We needed our oil

Because we didn't want
Those electric cars.

At one time there were
Huge monsters that

Walked where we walk,
Nature swallowed them easy.

Or maybe you believe
It all started with Adam and Eve,

But they too were kicked
From the garden

As are we,
With our poison beaches

Run down towns
And our atmosphere

That kills.
I write a poem

And preach to the converted.
We send out loud messages

To ourselves,
That our world is dying:

1984, Blade Runner,
Armageddon, The Road.

I've yet to read a book,
Or watch a film about a future

I'd like to live in.
Fortunately for me,

I'll die before the earth,
But I'd like a place for my

Computer chip self
To click and beep

In bright, clean happiness.

VENICE

We went out to Venice for a *stay-cation,*
I've been working too much and needed

To relax. We took *Gone Girl* and read
On the beach, between the graffiti wall

And the lifeguard post near the rocks
That go out in the water like a dragon tail.

Maybe Nick Dunn killed his wife, *Amazing
Amy,* or maybe it's all a game she set up.

One day we did a script reading for a movie
About Ken Kesey and the Merry Pranksters,

The next day we did one about young Tenn
Williams and the young days that inspired

His first masterpiece: *The Glass Menagerie.*
Monday morning I met with Bruce T. Cheung

On the basketball court that was used
In *White Men Can't Jump,* or *American History X,*

Or both, just a little way down from Arnold's
Muscle Beach. We talked about our film,

Zeroville, which is about Hollywood
In the seventies. We talked about *Salò:*

120 Days of Sodom, and *A Place in the Sun.*

*

Bruce and I got breakfast; he got a
Walt Whitman Omelet (crispy bacon),

The Faulkner Omelet had ham
And avocados and Gouda.

At the bookstore next door;
I got Styron's *Nat Turner,* and Bruce

Got one by a guy who is a friend of Dean
Bakoupolus who wrote *Please Don't Come*

Back From the Moon, which we're adapting
Into a film—it's about absent fathers,

Told through a mysterious phenomenon
Where all the dads in town just leave,

And the teen boys are forced to be the men.
We talked about how to make the end work.

Then I said, "I came here when I was fourteen
For YMCA Surf Camp, but no one could actually surf.

We almost got kicked out for being stupid."
It had been my first time in Los Angeles,

Now I've been here almost twenty years.

As the sun set, we watched skaters in the bowl.
This one black kid: tall, thin, fun, at perfect ease on the board,

Sailed around the bowl trying to perfect a trick:
To catch a football in a midair move.

He never got it, but kept practicing, unto dark.

HELLO WOMAN

Hello woman, I'd like to be you.
Not because I don't enjoy my man
Body, my man strength, my man looks,
My man mind, but because I love yours

Even more. I love your woman body
I love your woman mind,
Your woman face that is delicate,
And even has a little downy hair.

I love the shapely soft parts,
I love the vagina lips, no cock,
I love the butt swoop, and the clean
Butthole in the middle.

I love the woman bond,
So much more than the man.
I love the woman desires,
The love, the strength, the connection

More. More, more, more.
The man is angry, the man
Is destructive, the man wants more.
The woman *is* more, the woman is all.

If I ever got high, it would be to be
The woman. If I ever did porn,
I'd want to be the woman.
I don't want to be the man *in* woman

I just want to be woman.
But I will never be woman.
I am man, trapped in man.
I have no escape from this body,

This mind, this upbringing.
My only escape is a poem,
Feel the curves
They are the liquid shape

Of my woman body.

NEW REBEL

Rebel, rebel, *rebel.*

*

There is a way to be, and then there is a way to be boring.

*

When I think of "rebel" I think of James Dean in *Rebel Without a Cause.* But then I think of all the lazy journalists who have used James Dean to identify or denigrate some new up-and-coming actor, and I see that the image of Dean has been tarnished.

*

I think of Dean's ghost shooting through his windshield with the inertia of his Porsche, Spyder, racing down the dusty road to Salinas, right before impact with old Donald Turnupseed's dinky sedan—"He's got to see us," said Dean, to his passenger, Rolf Wütherich, his mechanic, right before impact—but he didn't see them, and then, POW. Dean's ghost never stopped, launched from that moment, off the back of his image, and shot through every generation after.

*

It shot through the outlaw antics of Dennis Hopper—
"motorcycles man, I got that from Dean, man."
Shot through the slouchy insouciant pose and attitude of Bobby Dylan.
Shot through the jazzy heroin rhythms of Chet Baker.
Shot through the fuck-you-punch to the art world of cigarette smoking Jackson Pollock—he crashed too, didn't he?
Shot through the siren of the streets, Jean-Michel Basquiat.
Shot through the blue jeans of the working class hero, Bruce Springsteen.
Shot through the art films of Kenneth Anger—*Scorpio Rising,* Dean lives, hail Satan.

Shot through the vampire teen phenomenon of Robert Pattinson, and even more so in his hard core ex, Kristen Stewart, a brooding Dean if I ever saw one.
Shot through Jack Kerouac and Neal Cassady out on the road.
Shot through Terrence Malick—"I'll kiss your ass if he don't look like James Dean."

*

The ghost, it shot through, and inhabited, and the Dean influence grew, like a phantom.

*

That's the problem with idols, they become communal, and the lame and boring take them for their own purposes. How can you be dangerous in the age when MTV appropriates all youth rebellion and commercializes it? Of course there is still rebellious stuff on MTV but it is all framed by the network.

*

Social networking is a fresh road of access. It's scary to magazines and newspapers because it spells their doom. The digital writing is on the wall and they decry it in the old fashioned writing of ink on glossy pages and newsprint.

*

I hate a selfie as much as anyone. But I love a selfie more than anyone. Know why? Because it's mine. And yours is yours. It is taken in that special place between self and mirror. If it's a true selfie it is held by the subject, so that the arm is circling out in front of the person, and the camera is just an extension of the self. Like an octopus tentacle with an eye at the end looking back at its body.

*

Group, group, group. We all live in a group. The citadels are crumbling. New ways of standing above will be developed, eventually, but for now the old ways are crumbling.

*

The rebels of a new generation where everything can be stolen and reposted? Those that steal and collage and repost in the most interesting ways.

*

The Bling Ringers, those teens who stole all that shit from Lindsay Lohan, and Paris Hilton, they are the punk rockers of to-day. Of course they're douche bags, and of course we don't like them, but who liked Punks back in the day? They were the out-siders: the smelly, and the ugly. Not the punks appropriated by children's television today, softened by MTV, but the ugly shits who shot up heroin mixed with toilet water. They weren't cool, but they were rebels.

*

The Bling Ringers are pretty, but they're criminals. They're MTV on the surface, and Sid Vicious underneath.

*

Richard Ramirez, "The Night Stalker," who would break into people's homes, kill the male in his sleep and rape the women, no matter how old—sometimes grandmas—started as a burglar. He would break into houses to steal items for drugs, then, later, instead of just stealing, he started killing the people inside. Hail Satan.

*

Rebellion involves violence. A killing.

*

Sometimes violence is more stomachable when it is cloaked in comedy. You can kill people with no repercussions as long as they're laughing.

*

Today, there are two types of rebels: those that fight the system outright, and those that walk the line between acceptance of the system, and destruction of the system. If you're on the inside (I'm on the inside of the Hollywood system) you can work your rebellion into your work without seeming to rebel. This is *my* kind of rebellion.

*

Oz and *Spring Breakers* out at the same time.
And *Interior. Leather Bar* out at the same time too. Real gay sex.
Milk and *Pineapple Express* out in the same year.
Teaching graduate film at the best film schools in the country and posting shirtless selfies.

*

I love you, I love you, I love you, I love you.

LANA POEM ESSAY

This is a poem about Lana Del Rey.

*

This is an essay about Lana Del Rey.

*

Lana has become my friend. She is a musician who is a poet and a video artist.

*

She grew up on the East Coast but she is an artist of the West Coast.

*

When I watch her stuff, when I listen to her stuff, I am reminded of everything I love about Los Angeles. I am sucked into a long gallery of Los Angeles cult figurines, and cult people, up all night like vampires, and into the sunrise like bikers.

*

The only difference between Lana and me is her haunting voice. That carries everything. The voice is the central axle around which the spokes of everything else extend.

*

My axle, like her voice is for her, is my acting. Out of it, I do everything else.

*

I don't like vampires, or bikers in my life, but I like them in my art.

*

Lana lives in her art, and when she comes down to earth for interviews, it gets messy, because she isn't made for this earth. She is made to live in the world she creates. She is one who has been so disappointed by life, she had to create her own world. Just let her live in it.

*

I am a performer and she is a performer.

*

The thing about singers, especially the ones who write their own lyrics, is that everyone reads the person into the songs. An actor is sometimes aligned with his roles, but a singer is asked about her lyrics as if they were direct statements of her true thoughts and feelings.

*

Sometimes Lana doesn't know what to say in interviews, so she plays into the idea that her songs are her, and not her creations.

*

Lana spends a lot of time alone because everyone wants in.

*

She has this idea for a film. I want to do it because it's a little like *Sunset Boulevard*. A woman is alone in a big house in LA. She doesn't want to go out. She starts to go crazy, and becomes paranoid because she feels like people are watching her. Even in her own house. It's like an awesome B movie that lives in Lana's head. It's about her, and it's not about her. Just like her music.

*

I wanted to interview Lana for a book and she said, "Just write around me, it's better if it's not my own words. It's almost better if you don't get me exactly, but try."

BORN TO DIE

My little apartment in Los Feliz,
Said to once be owned by Charlie
Chaplin, but you know, they say that
About all the apartments in LA.

I dream about Lana Del Rey,
And she dreams about Lana Del Rey,
And is Lana Del Rey, a dream
She created and then entered.

(Will she enter the dream forever?)

In my little apartment I have my pot
And my wigs, and my make up,
That I apply slowly, in slow motion,
In my Marilyn mirror with the star lights,

And "Born to Die" on repeat,
And a tiger-orange fire in the background,
In my little mind, within my unsheathed
Head, shaved and naked, for now.

(I've entered the dream and killed reality.)

Nathanael West's Hollywood painting
Was a raging, Bosch-like, conflagration,
Full of his denizens on the outskirts:
Out of work cowboys, extras, unfunny comedians,

All screaming, and burning,
And also fanning the flames;
As they buttfucked, and sucked
In every room of all the Mansions.

In the Hollywood of the mind.

BROTHER ONE

This brother, Tom, once
Told me, on a family vacation—

After everyone had moved
Out, and we reunited only twice

Annually: summer in Hilton Head
And Christmas in Palo Alto—

That he was sad because once
We were close. That we had done

All together, and he was always
Looking up to his big brother.

And then, he said, I left,
And we were no longer close.

"When?" I said. "When I went
To UCLA?" "No," he said.

"When you went to Kindergarten."

                    *

Sometimes two brothers split.
Their looks are so similar

They could be twins,
But inside, one takes the dark

Road, and one takes the light.
Tom followed my father

Into Oakland spirituality,
I didn't go. I walked

Into the land of Hollywood,
Where Tom didn't want to go.

Now our father is dead,
Tom meditates alone.

I am all that my brother has
Decided he is not. But I love

This brother. I'm all he's got.

BROTHER TWO

Brother Two is the one who is more like me.

*

Not in looks so much as Brother One; but we do share a certain smile, a crinkle of the eye, and the sound of our laughs.

*

There are probably myriad little things we both do, handed down through DNA, and from proximity to the love of the same parents.

*

I try not to look for these things, because I'll think that they're mine, and that he has stolen them.

*

Brother Dave is the youngest by far. Seven years after me, and five after Tom.

*

When he was in High School in Palo Alto, I was long gone to Los Angeles.

*

By the time he graduated, I was Spider-Man's best friend.

*

Later he followed me to LA.

*

I went to UCLA, he went to USC.
He likes sports, I don't have time.
He's pretty short, but he has blond hair.
We both love cats, raised on them.

*

There was a time he and I went to the Bruin-Trojan football
     game.
USC was rated number one, but our quarterback ran the ball in
     three times.
The ride home, with Davy, and all his USC friends...was awk-
     ward.

*

He seems to not have a care in the world.
He is in funny movies,
And yes, he works very hard,
But I've never seen him cry.

*

He has a girlfriend, and they're very much in love.

*

It must be hard to have a brother who was in *Freaks and Geeks*
while you were still in *real* high school.

*

It must be hard to live in a body full of mannerisms, and with a
mind full of thoughts that I have already shown to the world.

40

*

For years in Hollywood he was *James Franco's little brother*.

*

He lived with me for a while, near Sunset, in the building Bette Davis died in. I gave him the bed, and he slept with the cats, *my* cats, Harry and Arturo. He fed them, and wooed them to his side.

*

For years he kept his distance.
I offered him roles in artistic things.
He turned me down.
His own brother.

*

He was running fast, away from my shadow.

*

When he moved out of the Bette Davis place, the cats went with him. I let them all go, with my everlasting love.

*

Now the brothers don't live together, but the brother cats still do.

THREE BROTHERS

We were raised by a mother
Who loved us, and a father

Who showed us strange strength.
We learned to love animals,

So as adults we
All keep them as pets.

We learned to love art,
Now that's how

We spend our lives:
Actor, Artist, Actor.

Every Christmas we come
Together, there are no

Children, so we give love
To each other; that's what

We were taught.
Our father is now gone

But the tradition lives on.
Merry Christmas to me,

Merry Christmas to Mom,
Merry Christmas Dave,

Merry Christmas Tom.

TWENTY-YEAR CHIP

Twenty years ago, today,
I took my last drink of King Alcohol.

Breaking probation
After school:

Ken's dad's liquor in Ken's backyard,
With Luke, Ivan, Beau, Matt 'n Mike.

When Ken's mom came home
We jumped the fence

And into my father's
Hand-me-down Honda Accord,

A jumble of bodies on the road,
Over to Matt's on Christmas Tree Lane.

But Beau had forgotten his weed.

On my way back with Beau,
The Accord went through a stop

On Middlefield Road, and a car
Slammed into our front,

Spinning the Accord.
I chose to drive away,

First a side street,
—letting Beau out—

And then a roundabout way
Back home, where

The cops were waiting.
I was made a ward of the court.

*

Ivan jumped from a parking
Garage in San Francisco;

Luke is in a rock band;
Ken lives in Japan;

Beau, I don't know; drunk driving,
Mike lost his license at age thirty-five.

I've addicted myself to other things
Like imagination, coffee, and sex.

I put the crazy man I was
Into the crazy men I play;

Acting is my drinking,
Movies are my drugs.

STRAIGHT JAMES/GAY JAMES

Straight James: Hey, bud, this is weird. You're interviewing yourself.

Gay James: Yeah, I know. Who's doing the interview, and who's being interviewed?

SJ: Let's just have a convo, and we'll both try to get to the bottom of James.

GJ: Okay, deal. But my question is, who is the real James, and who is the mask?

SJ: I guess that's what everyone wants to know, right?

GJ: I guess, but I also guess that even though I have this public persona that is all wacked out and hard to pin down, or annoying, or whatever, in some ways I'm still more real than if I were just hiding behind a façade or whatever.

SJ: Façade. Meaning, like, a movie-star façade?

GJ: Yeah, if I were to just hide behind my movies, and try to look cool, and don't talk about anything of substance, and just give bland answers to everything like an athlete. "Yeah, we played with heart out there tonight. Really brought it."

SJ: OK, so, good place to start. Let's get substantial: are you fucking gay or what?

GJ: Well, I like to think that I'm gay in my art and straight in my life. Although, I'm also gay in my life up to the point of intercourse, and then you could say I'm straight. So I guess it depends on how you define gay. If it means whom you have sex with, I guess I'm straight. In the twenties and thirties, they used to define homosexuality by how you acted and not by whom you slept with. Sailors would fuck guys all the time, but as long as they behaved in masculine ways, they weren't considered gay. I wrote a little poem about it.

GAY NEW YORK

Gay New York
Is the name of a book
About Gays in New York.
From the nineteenth century on.

Back in the thirties
Before the Second World War,
"Gay" wasn't even a word,
Unless you meant "happy."

You were "queer"
If you acted queer.
But you could turn a sailor
And still be straight

As long as you didn't speak
With a lisp or wear a dress.
Funny how a concept can change
A whole culture.

We have to worry
About who we have sex with.
Weird how one little blowjob
Will make you a fag nowadays.

SJ: Yeah, Hart Crane fucked a lot of those sailors.

GJ: OK, Hart Crane…so, when you played him in the film you directed, *The Broken Tower*, you fellate a dildo on-screen and then have simulated sex with Michael Shannon. What's up with that?

SJ: What's up with that? Well, I wanted those scenes to be explicit, for two reasons. One, I knew that Crane was an openly gay man in a time when that was rare, and he was so up front about it he scared his more conservative poetry friends, so those scenes were a way to parallel the in-your-face nature of Crane's own sexuality. I also knew that the movie was going to be full of dense poetry, so I wanted to break it up a bit with some hot sex.

GJ: Okay, but didn't you know that that would be the only thing the reviewers would talk about?

SJ: Of course, but that's their shortsightedness. And once I went to film school and started directing my own movies, I realized that I was going to direct only movies that I really cared about in ways that I wanted, regardless of critique. As an actor I have been in huge blockbusters like *Spider-Man* and *Planet of the Apes*, and in critical hits like *Milk* and *127 Hours*, as well as in successful comedies like *Pineapple Express* and *This Is the End*, so I know all sides of success. But when directing my own projects, the primary focus is the art. Yes, I want people to see them, and, sure, I'd like people to like them, but my primary allegiance is to the work itself.

GJ: Okay, whatever you say. But you're also a goofball, especially on your Instagram account. Do you want people to think you're gay? Wouldn't it be a good thing if you were just a straight dude, like Ryan Gosling, just straight and cool?

SJ: Why would you say that it was a good thing that people would consider me straight? I actually like it when people think I'm gay; it's a great shield. Like the guy in *Shampoo* or the play that *Shampoo* is based on, *The Country Wife* by Wycherley.

GJ: What do you mean? You want to be able to go around screwing other people's wives by pretending to be gay?

SJ: No. I guess I mean that I like my queer public persona. I like that it's so hard to define me and that people always have to guess about me. They don't know what the hell is up with me, and that's great. Not that I do what I do to confuse people, but as long as they are confused, I get time to play.

GJ: Some people think it's annoying.

SJ: If I'm so annoying, why do they write about me? If they were truly sick of my shit, they would just ignore me, but they don't. I don't do what I do for attention; I do it because I believe in what I do. Of course, some of it is tongue-in-cheek, but that's just a tonal thing. It's not like I call the paparazzi on myself or anything like that; I'm just having a conversation with the public. If you don't want to be part of the convo, check out. If you do, cool.

GJ: Okay, but some people tell you to just screw a guy, and then you'd get over all this gay art stuff, like playing the gay poet Hart Crane or another gay poet, Allen Ginsberg, or directing the movie *Interior. Leather Bar*, which has actual gay sex in it, or painting paintings of Seth Rogen naked. Maybe if you just fucked a guy, you'd get over all this exoticizing of gay lifestyles?

SJ: Maybe sex with a guy would change things, but I doubt it. Like I said, I'm gay in my art. Or, I should say, queer in my art. And I'm not this way for political reasons, although sometimes it becomes political, like when I voted for same-sex marriage, etc. But what it's really about is making queer art that destabilizes ingrained ways of being, art that challenges hegemonic thinking.

GJ: But inevitably people will think that you're gay; they will think that you're in *Milk*, and *Howl*, and *The Broken Tower*, and *Interior. Leather Bar* because you are actually gay. That all these projects are ways of playing gay hide-and-seek.

SJ: These are all works of art, and art is free; art is its own realm. Of course, they can be read through a biographical lens and, of course, something like *Interior. Leather Bar* uses my persona to talk about some of these very issues, but they are still works of art and not exactly nonfictional statements about who I am.

GJ: Is this interview a nonfictional statement about who you are?

SJ: Yes and no. Yes, in the sense that I am answering as James Franco, but no in the sense that it is a public statement in an entertainment magazine, which means that it is part of my public persona and not my private veridical self—and even if it were in the *New York Times*, it would be the same; it would be an expression of my public self.

GJ: Well, why don't you stop playing games and give us a little of your private self?

SJ: Kind of impossible, don't you think? As soon as I share it, it becomes public. Here's a little poem back at ya.

FAKE

> There is a fake version of me,
> And he's the one that writes
> These poems.
> He has an attitude and swagger
>
> That I don't have.
> But on the page, this fake me
> Is the me that speaks.
> And this fake me is louder
>
> Than the real me, and he
> Is the one that everyone knows.
> He's become the real me
> Because everyone treats me
>
> Like I'm the fake me.

GJ: And why is the public self any less sincere than the private self?

SJ: That's a good question. I guess, for me, I've disowned it a little bit. When I was young, I tried so hard to control the public's perception of me, but I found that to be a waste of energy, partly because I couldn't control how people saw me and partly because I stopped caring.

GJ: You don't care if people don't like you?

SJ: Sure, I care, but I don't let that stop me from doing something I believe in. And let's say all my fans suddenly turned against me overnight. If I were to be honest, I couldn't complain, because I've had an awesome life so far. I've had a life many people dream about, and if it went away tomorrow, I could still say I had my share of the good stuff.

GJ: Is that why you teach? To give back some of the good stuff to others?

SJ: Duh.

GJ: Want to elaborate on that?

SJ: Sure. I teach to stop thinking about myself for a bit. But also because I find the classroom to be a very pure place, largely un-affected by the business world. I like people who still dream big, who are consumed by their work. And that's how most students in MFA programs are.

GJ: Okay, last question. What do you say to people who criticize you for appropriating gay culture for your work?

SJ: I say fuck off, but I say it gently. This is such a fraught issue, and I am sensitive to all its aspects. But first of all, I was not the one who pulled my public persona into the gay world; that was the straight gossip press and the gay press speculating about me. I really don't care what people think about my sexuality, and it's also none of their business. So I really don't choose to identify with my public persona. I am not interested in most straight male-bonding rituals, but I am also kept from being fully em-braced by the gay community because I don't think anyone truly believes I have gay sex.

GJ: Oh, some do, believe me.

SJ: Well, good, I like that.

GJ: Why?

SJ: Because it means that I can be a figure for change. I am a figure who can show the straight community that many of their definitions are outdated and boring. And I can also show the gay community that many of the things about themselves that they are giving up to join the straight community are actually valuable and beautiful.

GJ: Okay, can we talk about *Child of God* for a minute? You adapted the Cormac McCarthy novel, and your buddy Scott Haze gives an amazing performance that's already been singled out by the *New York Times*.

SJ: Yup.

GJ: So, what the hell, James? Necrophilia? This dude is out in the woods having relationships with dead people! Everyone is going to think you're more crazy than they already do.

SJ: Well, let's remember that it's a faithful adaptation of a book by Cormac McCarthy, who won the Pulitzer and was in Oprah's Book Club. But you're right; it's grizzly material. But I didn't make the film because I was interested in sex with dead bodies; I did it because I was interested in who we are when we are alone and who we are when we're intimate with another person. Lester Ballard is a character who has full relationships with corpses—meaning he fills in both sides of the mental relationship, but he gets a body to interact with.

GJ: Sort of like this conversation with yourself, except there is only one body.

SJ: Shit, I'd love to fuck you. Would that make me gay?

GJ: You jerk me off all the time.

SJ: Yeah, but I'm thinking about women when I do it, or watching straight porn.

GJ: So, I know tons of gay guys who watch straight porn.

SJ: Anyway, this interview is going a little south, and I don't think my publicist will appreciate us talking about porn.

GJ: FINE, whatever, one more question.

SJ: You said the other question was the last.

GJ: Well, you have a lot of fucking projects to promote, and your publicist wants you to talk about all of them.

SJ: Don't tell me what my publicist wants.

GJ: Why not? She's my publicist too.

SJ: Yeah, but she wants you to stay out of the public eye because you're gay.

GJ: That's bullshit. Robin Baum doesn't give a shit what I do.

SJ: I don't know about that, but anyway, what's your question?

GJ: Tell me about this new film directed by Justin Kelly, one of the editors from *Milk*.

SJ: Basically, it's about this guy, Michael Glatze, who was this huge gay activist in San Francisco in the early 2000s who worked for *XY* magazine and would go around to high schools telling kids it was okay to be gay. And then he had this huge turn-around, and found God, and then became Christian, and then was ordained as a Christian minister, and now he's married to a woman. At first he turned on his ex-boyfriend and all his friends and said that if you're gay, you're going to hell. But I think he's since pulled back from that stance a little.

GJ: Well, that's nice of him.

SJ: Ha, yeah, he went a little extreme for a minute.

GJ: Hmmm, and why did he go straight?

SJ: He thought he was going to die.

GJ: And why are you gay?

SJ: Because it's more fun.

GJ: And why would you make that movie? I mean, what's the point?

SJ: Well, it's not as if it's a movie that is itself anti-gay. It's just a very interesting and unique way to examine the way that straight and gay are defined by others, and how we define ourselves.

GJ: (thinks for a minute) You know, you're pretty arrogant.

SJ: Why do you say that?

GJ: I don't know, this whole interview. Like, how dare you interview yourself? And it's just so annoying because you're always trying to be so meta, like in *This Is the End*.

SJ: Dude, this interview wasn't my idea. I was asked by this magazine to interview myself. And I didn't write *This Is the End*, but I'm glad I was in it. It was a way to talk about a lot of stuff without being threatening because it was comedic.

GJ: Okay, let's kiss in the mirror again.

SJ: You got it, baby.

(They kiss.)

BILDUNGSROMANS AND BILDUNGSROMANS

What is it to be in high school?
What to watch high school
On television, and in the movies?
I hated high school while in it,

But as I grew older I realized
It was the most important period,
It was the period when I found
Everything I loved, and still do:

Literature, art, acting, filmmaking.

High school is ages
Fourteen to eighteen,
When puberty hits its stride
And bodies are the sweetest.

Sex in high school
Is the most forbidden,
And I think the best,
The participants don't know the moves

But the act is framed by sweet evil.

If you look at many novels
That are regarded as works of maturity
You'll find that they actually deal with *youth*,
And the same old issues on the school yard:

Jonathan Franzen books, Richard Russo,
Stephen King, even *East of Eden*;
There is a reason
We have a whole category: *Bildungsroman*.

Some artists' work never leave this brief
Period, or they come back to it, again and again:
Harmony Korine, Gus Van Sant, Larry
Clark, Richard Prince, Sofia Coppola,

Bruce Springsteen, Lana Del Rey, and me.
Youth is a dancer, dancing on a knife,
And below is fire that ages, and marks you.
The elders wait in the fire, looking up at

The cunts and cocks in full bloom.

ACKNOWLEDGMENTS

My thanks to the editors of the following journals where the following poems originally appeared: *The Guardian*: "I Was Born Into a World"; *V Magazine*: "Brother One," "Brother Two," "Three Brothers," "New Rebel," and "Lana Poem Essay"; *FourTwoNine Magazine*: "Straight James/Gay James"; *Vice Magazine*: "Black Death."

Thank you, Gregg Barrios for the continued support.

I have been blessed with the best poets as friends: Alan Shapiro, Tony Hoagland and Frank Bidart.

And thank you to Lana Del Rey for the inspiration and friendship.

ABOUT THE AUTHOR

 James Franco is an actor, director, writer, and visual artist. He is the author of two works of fiction, *Palo Alto* and *Actors Anonymous*, and two books that collage memoir, snapshots, poems, and artwork, *A California Childhood* and *Hollywood Dreaming*. His poetry has appeared in a chapbook, *Strongest of the Litter*, and the book, *Directing Herbert White*. His writing has also been published in *Esquire*, the *Huffington Post*, *McSweeney's*, *N+1*, *Vanity Fair*, *The New York Times* and the *Wall Street Journal*. He has received MFAs in fiction from Brooklyn College and Columbia, an MFA in film from New York University, an MFA in art from Rhode Island School of Design, and an MFA in poetry from Warren Wilson College.

Franco's film appearances include *Milk*, *Pineapple Express*, *This is the End*, *Spring Breakers*, *Oz*, and *127 Hours*, which earned him an Academy Award nomination. He portrayed poets Allen Ginsberg in the film *Howl*, C.K. Williams in *The Color of Time*, and Hart Crane in *The Broken Tower*, a film Franco adapted and directed. He has also adapted many poems into films that he has directed, including short films based on "Herbert White" by Frank Bidart, the collection *Black Dog, Red Dog* by Stephen Dobyns, "The Clerk's Tale" by Spencer Reece, and "The Feast of Stephen" by Anthony Hecht. Franco has also adapted to film the novels *As I Lay Dying*, and *Sound and the Fury* by William Faulkner, *Child of God* by Cormac McCarthy, *In Dubious Battle* by John Steinbeck, *The Long Home* by William Gay, and *Zeroville* by Steve Erickson.

He lives in New York and Los Angeles.

CPSIA information can be obtained at www.ICGtesting.com
Printed in the USA
BVOW05s0155270216

438295BV00011BA/253/P